CALCULATOR GAMES

by Michael Donner
illustrated by Lynn Matus

GOLDEN PRESS · NEW YORK
Western Publishing Company, Inc.
Racine, Wisconsin

Created and Produced by Tree Communications, Inc., New York
Managing Editor: J. Munves, Art Director: M. E. Gold
Design Assistants: T. Augusta, C. F. Jones

Library of Congress Catalog Card Number: 76-49714

FOREWORD

This book is designed for use with (and provides instructions for operating) any standard algebraic pocket calculator. Without exception, the inexpensive models currently sold are of this type. But if your children have a different type, such as the kind that uses reverse Polish notation (RPN) or the kind with more than one function sign on certain keys, you will have to show them how to work it.

TABLE OF CONTENTS

HOW TO WORK YOUR CALCULATOR

You can play all the games, do all the tricks, and solve all the puzzles in this book with any calculator that has room to show eight numbers when you press the keys. Of course, there are many kinds of calculators, but most types do all the basic steps in the same way. So, if you don't already know how to work your calculator, the instructions given here will explain everything you need to know to use it with this book.

The drawing to the left shows the keys that make a calculator work. Your calculator will probably **not** look exactly the same, but it will have the same keys on it somewhere. (The key marked **C** here is sometimes marked **C ALL**, **CLEAR**, **CA**, or **C/CE**.) Any extra keys your calculator may have will not be used. Your calculator also has a display where the numbers you push are shown. Turn the calculator on by flicking the "off-on" switch. A zero will appear on the display.

Try solving these four problems on your calculator:

$$2 \qquad 9 \qquad 4 \qquad 8)\overline{24}$$
$$+3 \qquad -6 \qquad \times 5$$

First, think of the problems as if they were written across the page:

$$2 + 3 = ? \qquad 9 - 6 = ? \qquad 4 \times 5 = ? \qquad 24 \div 8 = ?$$

(In division problems, be sure to put the number you are dividing before the division sign.)

Next, press the keys in the order in which the numbers and signs are written. For the first problem, start by pressing the **2** key. After you press it, the display will look like this:

Next, press the "plus" (**+**) key. The display looks the same, but the machine is now ready to add.

Now, press the **3** key. The **2** will disappear and the display will look like this:

Finally, press the "equals" **(=)** key, and the answer will appear.

To start a new calculation, press the key marked **C** to erase, or clear, the display of the previous calculation.

Now, do the second problem like this:

The third problem is done like this:

The fourth problem, **24 ÷ 8**, is a little different because it has a number in it with two digits, 24. But again, all you have to do is press the keys in the order in which the problem is written:

To test yourself, try these problems:

9 + 7 = ?   **12 × 3 = ?**   **47 − 20 = ?**   **171 ÷ 19 = ?**
(Answer: 16)   (Answer: 36)   (Answer: 27)   (Answer: 9)

Other Symbols on the Calculator

If you look at the first calculator on the next page, you will see a key marked with a dot (·). That is the decimal point. It is used in a few games where fractions come up. Fractions are parts of whole numbers, just as cents are parts of a dollar. To do the problem: a dollar and 25 cents times 3 equals ?, you would press **1.25 × 3 =** . The answer is 3.75 or 3 dollars and 75 parts of another dollar. When the decimal point occurs on the display, the part of the answer to the left of the point is the whole number, and the part to the right of it is the fraction.

Two other symbols that sometimes come up on the display are shown below. To produce one of them, press **5 − 36 =**. The negative sign (−) that has appeared on the display means that the answer to the problem is less than zero. If this is hard to imagine, think of winter days in the north where the temperature sometimes falls **below zero**. Numbers below zero are called negative numbers. They are the exact opposite of numbers above zero. When you add to negative numbers they become smaller. When you subtract from them, they get larger.

To produce the other symbol on the display, try this problem: **10000000 × 10000000 = ?** The display will show an answer with a little circle, a star, a dot, or the letter **C** following it. On some calculators, the display will blink on and off. The form of the symbol varies from one calculator to another, but it always means that the real answer is too big to be shown on the display. This situation is called an overload. The machine stops there and, usually, the only command it will obey after that is **Clear**. Press **C**.

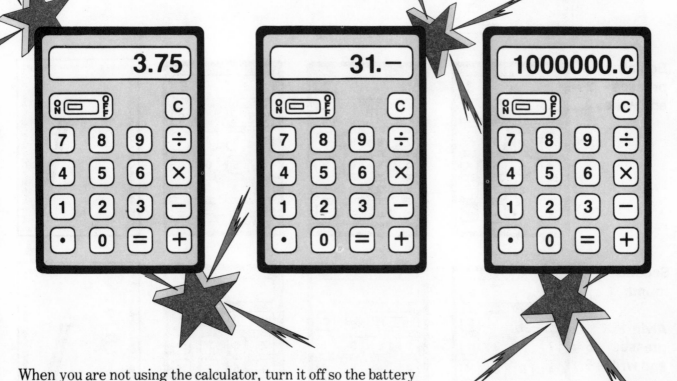

When you are not using the calculator, turn it off so the battery does not run down.

NUMBER WRESTLING

First round:

Alvin presses 3

and writes it down.

Here's a game two people can play with one calculator, paper, and pencil. The object is to reach a score of exactly 21 or else to force your opponent to go over 21. Five victories wins the match.

How to Play

Determine the order of the players for the first game by tossing a coin. In later games, take turns being first.

The first player presses any number from 1 to 9 and writes it down. The second player adds any other number from 1 to 9 and also writes it down. He may not play the number that the first player used. The two players continue in turn, adding on numbers that have not yet been used.

The player who brings the total to exactly 21, wins. But going over 21 loses. It is important to write down the used numbers so mistakes do not occur.

A sample game is shown here, starting at the top of the page. As the game starts, Alvin has won the toss and goes first.

Beulah presses + 2 = and writes 2.

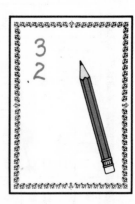

Second round:

Alvin presses + 5 = and writes 5.

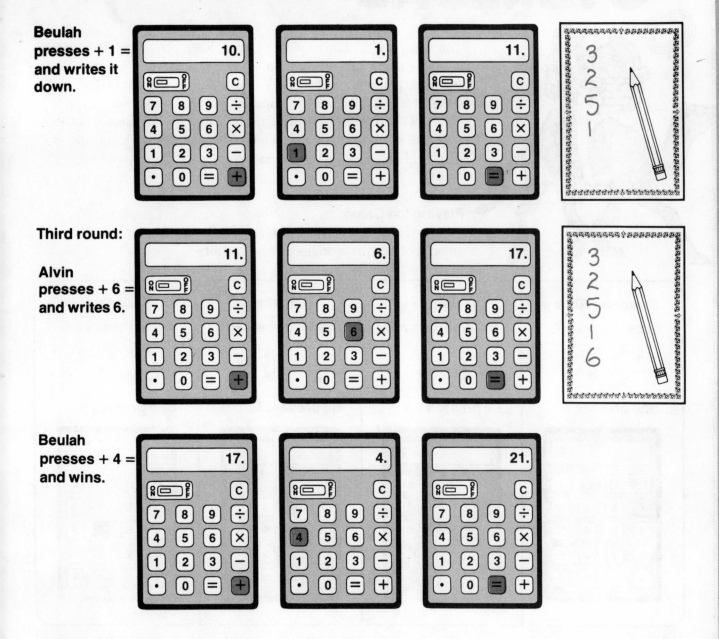

Beulah presses + 1 = and writes it down.

Third round:

Alvin presses + 6 = and writes 6.

Beulah presses + 4 = and wins.

Strategy: Alvin's last move cost him the game. Before his move, the total stood at 11, so 10 was needed to make 21. Only 4, 6, 7, 8 and 9 were left to be played. Of these numbers, the only combination that adds up to 10 is 4 and 6. If Alvin chose either the 4 or the 6 he would lose, because Beulah could then pick the other and bring the total to 21, which she did. Alvin should have picked 7, 8, or 9. Then Beulah would have had to go over 21.

OVERLOAD

This is a game for two or more players. Each player should have his own calculator, and all the calculators should have a display with the same amount of numbers. You will also need a pair of dice, and if there is only one calculator, paper and pencil to keep score. The object of the game is to be the first to get such a high score that the overload symbol, explained on page 7, appears on your calculator display. Each overload counts as 1 point; and 5 points wins the match.

Playing the Game:
To see who goes first, each player rolls the dice and enters the total amount of his throw on his own calculator.

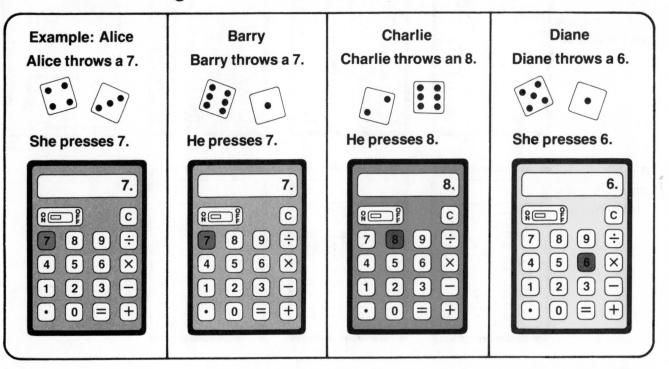

Example: Alice
Alice throws a 7.

She presses 7.

7.

Barry
Barry throws a 7.

He presses 7.

7.

Charlie
Charlie throws an 8.

He presses 8.

8.

Diane
Diane throws a 6.

She presses 6.

6.

If there are no ties at this point, the player with the highest number goes first, the next-highest goes second, and so on. But if there are any ties, **all** players roll the dice again and add their new throw to their previous total. Play continues in this way until everyone has a different number on his calculator display.

Example:
In the sample just given, Alice and Barry were tied at 7, so everyone must roll the dice again. It makes no difference that Charlie had an 8.

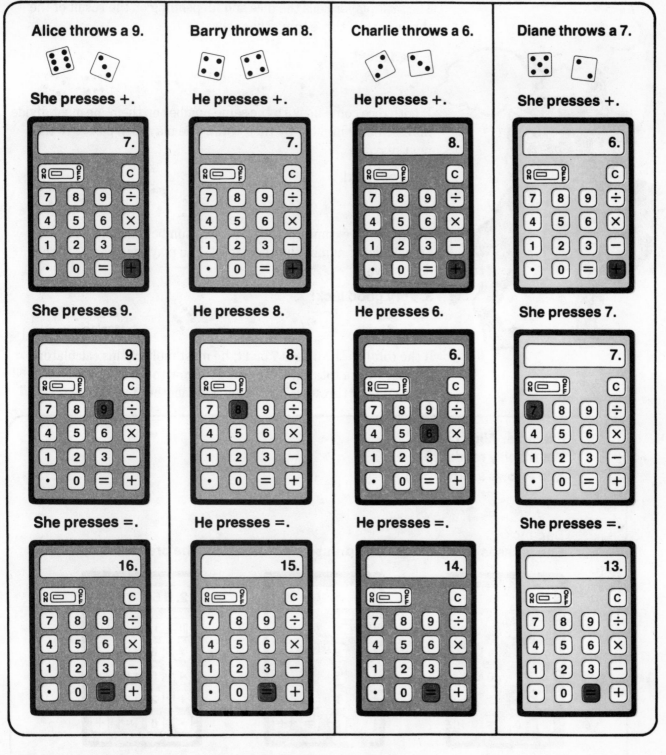

Alice throws a 9.

She presses +.

She presses 9.

She presses =.

Barry throws an 8.

He presses +.

He presses 8.

He presses =.

Charlie throws a 6.

He presses +.

He presses 6.

He presses =.

Diane throws a 7.

She presses +.

She presses 7.

She presses =.

There are no longer any ties, so the game can go on to the next stage. The order of the players is: Alice, Barry, Charlie, and then Diane, the same order the players appear in on this page.

The first player rolls the dice and, depending on the result of the throw, one of three things happens:

1. Bad luck!

If both dice come up with the same number on them, he must divide his calculator number by their total. The play then passes to the next player.

2. Good luck!

If the two dice come up with different numbers, he must multiply his calculator number by their total. The play then passes to the next player.

3. Very good luck!

If the total on the dice is 7 or 11, he must multiply his calculator number by the total AND he gets to throw the dice again. Every time a player throws a 7 or 11, he wins another free turn.

Example: Alice begins.
Her display reads: 16.
She throws a 6 (two 3s!).

Bad luck.
She presses ÷

She presses 6.

She presses =.

(Alice's new score, 2.6666666, may look like a big number, but it is really just a bit more than 2, and much less than she started with.)

Barry goes second.
His display reads: 15.
He also throws a 6,
but not a double.

 Good luck.

He presses ×.

He presses 6.

He presses =.

His score, 90, is a good one for the first round. He passes the dice to Charlie.

By now, you will be able to follow these examples on your own calculator without the help of pictures.

Charlie goes third. His display reads: 14.
He throws a 7. Very good luck.
He presses ×. He presses 7. He presses =. And gets: 98.
And now he goes again. He throws an 11. Very good luck again.
He presses × 11 =. And his score is: 1078.
And now he goes once again. He throws a 9, and after multiplying again, his total has quickly grown to 9702. Finally he passes the dice to Diane.

Diane goes last. Her display reads: 13. She throws the dice, enters her score, and when her turn is over, she passes the dice back to Alice.

As you can see by the sample scores, the numbers rise and fall quickly, and runs of good or bad luck can turn the tables at any time. Building a score of one hundred million (100,000,000) and thus causing an overload seldom takes more than a dozen rounds of play. An overload should be announced as soon as it occurs. A new game begins immediately, and all players start again from zero.

SMARTER THAN YOU THINK

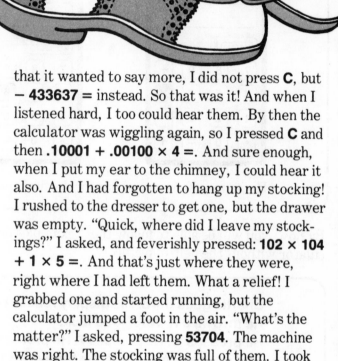

By now, you have probably realized that your calculator is a whiz with numbers. But did you know it can also talk? To strike up a conversation, press: **200 − 16 × 42 + 6 ÷ 100 ÷ 100 =**. Then turn the calculator upside down to read the answer. Now that you know there's really somebody there, why don't you ask it its name? (Before asking a new question, it is good manners to press the clear key.) Press **C**, then press: **317 × 7 × 11 × 13 + 220 =**.

Calculator Riddles
If your calculator can answer questions, maybe it can solve riddles too. Like: What's white, round on top, flat on the bottom, cold on the outside, warm on the inside, and sometimes full of Eskimos? Press: **16 × 49 + 7 ÷ 10000 =**. What else is round and white, but looks like a zero? Press: **331 × 3 + .35009 =**.

If you thought that was fun, ask the calculator what it thinks you should do next: **379 × 7 × 11 × 13 + 540 =**. If it was boring, press: **7 × 7 × 7 × 7 × 2 + 113 =**. Were you amazed? Press: **2 × 3 × 5 × 5 × 5 + 1 × 2 × 3 + 3 =**.

A Mid-Winter's Tale
Calculators don't usually say much, but every once in a while, they say one thing after another. For instance, one Christmas Eve, my calculator (whose name is **7 × 5 × 10 × 11 + 9 × 2 =**) fell off the shelf and woke me up. It was obviously trying to tell me something. I hastily pressed: **5 + 1 × 5 × 5 − 3 × 5 + 3 × 5 + 1 × 5 × 5 × 5 + 30000 =**. I didn't exactly understand, but seeing that it wanted to say more, I did not press **C**, but **− 433637 =** instead. So that was it! And when I listened hard, I too could hear them. By then the calculator was wiggling again, so I pressed **C** and then **.10001 + .00100 × 4 =**. And sure enough, when I put my ear to the chimney, I could hear it also. And I had forgotten to hang up my stocking! I rushed to the dresser to get one, but the drawer was empty. "Quick, where did I leave my stockings?" I asked, and feverishly pressed: **102 × 104 + 1 × 5 =**. And that's just where they were, right where I had left them. What a relief! I grabbed one and started running, but the calculator jumped a foot in the air. "What's the matter?" I asked, pressing **53704**. The machine was right. The stocking was full of them. I took the other stocking instead, and hurried with it to the fireplace. We made it, but it was a close call.

Making Your Own Words
Would you like to make up other words on your calculator? It's easy. The letters you can use and the upside-down numbers that produce them are: **E (3); G (9 or 6); H (4); I (1); L (7); O (0); and S (5).** See what words you can make from these seven letters. For added interest, invent arithmetic problems that lead you to the correct answer. For example, if you make the word OIL, the upside-down number is 710. From there, it is not hard to make up problems such as **800 − 90 = ?** Then make up a riddle like: What saves us toil, is shiny as foil, and can cause a soil?

FACTS AND CALCULATIONS

Here's a chance to test your knowledge of basic facts and your skill in using a calculator at the same time. All you have to do is give the answer to one question. But, what a question! Before you try to do the calculations, be sure you have all the facts straight. If there are any things you aren't sure of, ask an older person or check an encyclopedia or almanac. When you think you have the final answer, double-check your facts and calculations, because one little slip will make the whole thing wrong.

The Question Is: What answer do you get when you go through all these steps, one after another, on the calculator:

a. Multiply the number of days in a leap year by the number of countries in South America (check a map),

b. Subtract the value of the Roman number MDCLXVI,

c. Add 0825, right side up and backwards,

d. Divide by the number of playing cards in a standard deck (not counting jokers),

e. Multiply by the year Christopher Columbus discovered America,

f. Fold a sheet of paper in half four times, open it up, and subtract the number of boxes that have been formed between the fold lines,

g. Divide by the number of pennies in $2.12,

h. Add the number of dwarfs in the story of Snow White,

i. Multiply **twice** by the number of letters in the alphabet,

j. Divide by the number of signs in the zodiac,

k. Subtract the year a man first walked on the moon,

l. Add 2000,

m. Subtract the number of days February usually has,

n. Add one-third the number of times the letter j appears on this page,

o. Divide by a gross (a dozen dozen),

p. Subtract the number of degrees in a circle,

q. Add the number of days in a fortnight,

r. And divide by the number of years in a century.

The answer is on page 48.

CALCULATOR MAZE

The number maze works like any ordinary maze. The object is to help the pig reach the corn by tracing a line from start to finish. But you can't take just any path. This is a highly intelligent porker. So, you must figure out which path has the correct answer to the calculator problems given along the way. You can read the numbers and signs up or down, to the left or right, and around corners. Get an answer, then check it on your calculator. A wrong answer means a wrong path. A right answer means you are on your way. Use a coin or a button to mark your path.

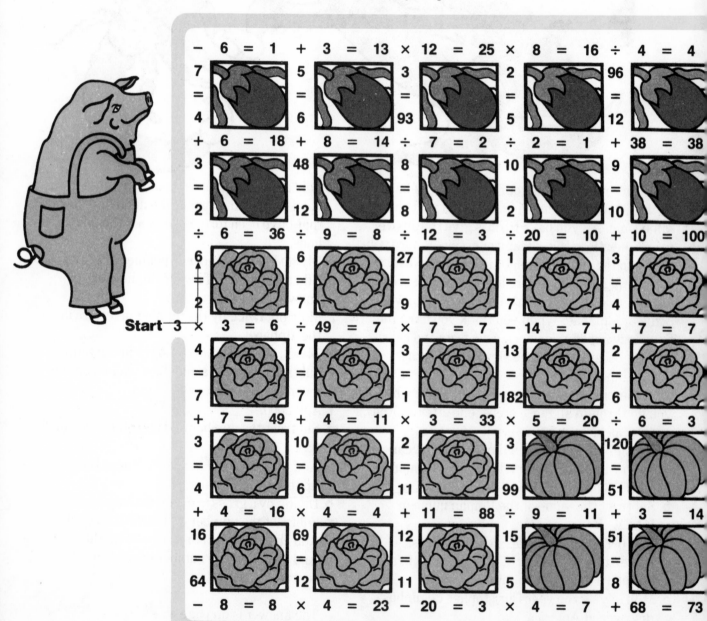

```
−   6  =  1   +   3  =  13   ×  12  =  25   ×   8  =  16   ÷   4  =   4
7              5              3              2              96
=              =              =              =              =
4              6              93             5              12
+   6  =  18   +   8  =  14   ÷   7  =   2   ÷   2  =   1   +  38  =  38
3              48             8              10             9
=              =              =              =              =
2              12             8              2              10
÷   6  =  36   ÷   9  =   8   ÷  12  =   3   ÷  20  =  10   +  10  = 100
6              6              27             1              3
=              =              =              =              =
2              7              9              7              4
Start 3 × 3  =   6   ÷  49  =   7   ×   7  =   7   −  14  =   7   +   7  =   7
4              7              3              13             2
=              =              =              =              =
7              7              1              182            6
+   7  =  49   +   4  =  11   ×   3  =  33   ×   5  =  20   ÷   6  =   3
3              10             2              3              120
=              =              =              =              =
4              6              11             99             51
+   4  =  16   ×   4  =   4   +  11  =  88   ÷   9  =  11   +   3  =  14
16             69             12             15             51
=              =              =              =              =
64             12             11             5              8
−   8  =   8   ×   4  =  23   −  20  =   3   ×   4  =   7   +  68  =  73
```

For example, at the start, the number 3 is given, and then a multiplication sign. At that point the path forks in three directions, each showing a different number, an equals sign, and an answer. If you take the bottom fork, you are saying 3 × 4 = 7, the middle fork 3 × 3 = 6, the top fork 3 × 2 = 6. Only one statement is correct, the one given in the top fork. So you can move the coin or button from START to the top fork and as far as the next fork, where a new choice must be made. Is it 6 ÷ 6 = 36 (right fork), or 6 ÷ 2 = 3 (top fork)? When you know, move the coin to the next fork, and so on. Now you are on your own. The correct path is shown on page 48.

70 = 47 ×   1 = 14 +   0 = 7 −   13 = 27 −   59 = 1 −

8 = 80   8 = 7   5 = 38   3 = 4   1 = 2

4 = 4 −   3 = 4 −   2 = 16 ×   84 = 7 +   100 = 83 ×

6 = 4   19 = 4   2 = 87   13 = 9   8 = 20

9 = 10 ÷   2 = 7 +   3 = 10 +   3 = 13 +   7 = 20 ÷

14 = 2   120 = 12   16 = 8   3 = 0   5 = 4

10 = 9 ÷   3 = 8 ×   1 = 1 ÷   1 = 1 +   1 = 2 −   4 = 0

28 = 2   11 = 11   12 = 7   48 = 96   4 = 8

6 = 4 ÷   22 = 6 ×   3 = 84 −   44 = 48 +   96 = 12 −

56 = 2   6 = 4   28 = 3   96 = 96   13 = 7

8 = 112 ÷   71 = 9 ×   10 = 31 ×   6 = 4 −   16 = 9 ×

7 = 4   8 = 7   98 = 99   4 = 4   0 = 1

2 = 3 +   68 = 23 ÷   64 = 32 −   16 = 8 ÷   4 = 2 −

17

QUIZ FOR NIMBLE FINGERS

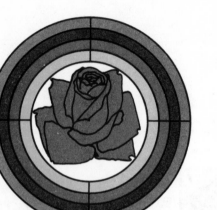

Want to test your accuracy with long strings of calculations? Try the tricky ones that follow. Jot your answers down on scratch paper and check them against the answers given on page 48. If you get 25 or more right, you're a whiz, and a score of 20 is pretty good. If you get less than 15 right, maybe you need to trim your fingernails.

Speed Games

How fast can you press all the keys you should, without pressing any you shouldn't—without making any mistakes? To find out, try the next two games.

1. Ring around the rosy: Run rings around the **5** key like this: First press **12369874** and **+**. Then advance one key along the circle to enter **23698741** and this time press **–**. Advance to **36987412** and switch back to **+**. Continue to advance around the circle, remembering to alternate between **+** and **–** after each ring. Make nine rings in all, ending with the same number you started with. Then press **=**. Written out, the problem reads: 12369874 + 23698741 – 36987412 + 69874123 – 98741236 + 87412369 – 74123698 + 41236987 – 12369874 =. Write your answer down.

2. Plowing the fields: Travel the rows on your keyboard like this: First move across, pressing: **123 × 654 × 789**; then go back, pressing: **÷ 987 ÷ 456 ÷ 321**; then go up, pressing: **+ 147 + 852 + 369**; then come back down, pressing: **– 963 – 258 – 741 =**. Write your answer down.

Math Jumbles

It's easy to do calculations if all you're doing is adding numbers to each other but what if the math signs are jumbled? Try these next two very carefully.

3. $1 + 2 - 3 \times 4 \div 5 + 6 - 7 \times 8 \div 9 = ?$

4. $9 \div 8 \times 7 - 6 + 5 \div 4 \times 3 - 2 + 1 = ?$ Write your answers down.

Breaking the Bank

Here are two problems in which the answer is not the important thing. What matters is how many steps it takes to get there.

5. If you were to press the sequence: $1 \times 2 \times 3 \times 4 \times 5 \times 6 \times 7 \times 8 \times 9 \times 10$ and so on, what would be the last number you press before the calculator overloads?

6. If you press the sequence: **1 + 2 × 3 + 4 × 5 + 6** and continue on into double-digits as above, what is the last number you can press before the calculator overloads?

Letter-Number Code

Solve the next group of problems, using the letter-number code at right:

A = 1	J = 10	S = 19
B = 2	K = 11	T = 20
C = 3	L = 12	U = 21
D = 4	M = 13	V = 22
E = 5	N = 14	W = 23
F = 6	O = 15	X = 24
G = 7	P = 16	Y = 25
H = 8	Q = 17	Z = 26
I = 9	R = 18	

Write the days of the week and the months of the year on a sheet of paper, putting them in number code, following the order shown below. Then using your calculator and working word by word, multiply the first letter by the second, divide by the third letter, add the fourth, subtract the fifth, and continue multiplying, dividing, adding, and subtracting each letter in turn until you come to the end of the word. Always follow the order × ÷ + −. In doing Sunday, for example, you would enter: **19 × 21 ÷ 14 + 4 − 1 × 25 =**. Fill in the answer you get for Sunday.

Now, using the same formula, get the totals for the rest of the days and months. Write the answers down opposite your code list.

7. Sunday = ?

8. Monday = ?

9. Tuesday = ?

10. Wednesday = ?

11. Thursday = ?

12. Friday = ?

13. Saturday = ?

14. January = ?

15. February = ?

16. March = ?

17. April = ?

18. May = ?

19. June = ?

20. July = ?

21. August = ?

22. September = ?

23. October = ?

24. November = ?

25. December = ?

26. Using the answers you got for the days of the week (Questions 7-13), multiply, divide, add, and subtract them in turn until you get the grand total for the week.

27. Using the answers you got for the months of the year (Questions 14-25), multiply, divide, add, and subtract them in turn until you get the grand total for the year. Ignore any minus signs in the previous answers.

Super-genius Questions:

28. It would take too long to do this problem, but take a guess at the answer: If you press the sequence: **1 + 2 + 3 + 4 + 5 + 6** and so on, pressing double-digits after you reach 10, what is the last number you would press before the calculator overloads? (You might actually try it, if you like counting sheep and that sort of thing.)

29. Another ambitious problem: If you press the sequence **1 − 2 ÷ 3 + 4 × 5 − 6 ÷ 7 + 8 × 9 − 10 ÷ 11 + 12 × 13**, and so on, what is the last number you would press before the calculator overloads?

MULTIPLICATION THE HARD WAY

There was once a cartoonist named Rube Goldberg who was famous for his drawings of ridiculously complicated methods for doing simple things. In his nutty world, turning a light on, for example, might happen this way: A monkey is hit on the head with a hammer, falls off a chair and onto a seesaw which bumps a pair of scissors which cuts a ribbon, causing a door to slam . . . and so on . . . until finally a small cannonball is fired to trip the switch that turns on the light.

Here is a way of turning any simple multiplication problem into just such a mess. The amazing thing is that you will come up with the right answer anyway!

Take a problem like 84 times 77. Instead of just pressing: **84 × 77 =** and arriving directly at the answer, as any normal person would do, try it this way:

1. Write one of the two numbers on a sheet of paper. Then use the calculator to divide it by 2 as many times as it takes to reach an answer of 1. Ignore any decimal fractions that result, and copy only the whole numbers that come up on the display in each step, writing them in a column beneath the original number. In the example given you would:

	Write:
Press:	84
84 ÷ 2 =	
(Answer: 42)	42
÷ 2 = (21)	21
÷ 2 = (10.5)	10
÷ 2 = (5.25)	5
÷ 2 = (2.625)	2
÷ 2 = (1.3125)	1

2. Now write the other number in the original multiplication problem next to the first number. **Multiply** it by 2 as many times as you divided the first number, and write the answer at each step alongside the answers to the division steps. In the example, you would:

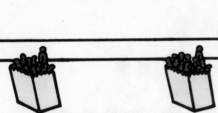

Press:	Write: 77		Your paper would then look like this:
77 × 2 =		84	77
(Answer: 154)	154	42	154
× 2 = (308)	308	21	308
× 2 = (616)	616	10	616
× 2 = (1232)	1232	5	1232
× 2 = (2464)	2464	2	2464
× 2 = (4928)	4928	1	4928

3. Cross out the even numbers in the first column as well as the numbers in the second column that are on the same line. (It doesn't matter whether the numbers in the second column are odd or even.) Your paper should then look like this:

~~84~~ - - - - - - - - ~~77~~
~~42~~ - - - - - - - - ~~154~~
21   308
~~10~~ - - - - - - - - ~~616~~
5   1232
~~2~~ - - - - - - - - ~~2464~~
1   4928

4. Add the numbers that remain in the second column only. In the example, you would:
Press: 308 + 1232 + 4928 =
(Answer: 6468)

As if miraculously, this is the correct answer for: 84 × 77. Check it by multiplying it yourself. You can use this method to amaze a friend . . . or just to check your homework.

21

HOW MANY SECONDS HAVE GONE BY SINCE YOU WERE BORN?

Most calculators have a display that is limited to eight digits. That doesn't seem like much, but few people ever use numbers that large in real-life calculations. Well, here's a chance to use eight digits and more in a real problem that has to do with you. The problem is to calculate how old you are . . . in seconds! And it will be easy if you follow 14 simple steps. (A three-step version that will give you a rough answer is given on page 24. The short method is quicker, of course, but the 14-step sequence is simple to follow and an adventure in itself. Whether you choose the long or the short way, make a guess at the answer before you begin. Write it down so you can compare it later with the real answer.)

Step 1: Copy the list of years at left. Draw a line under the year you were born and a second line above the present year. Count the number of years between the two lines you have drawn, and multiply this number by 365. Then count the number of Xs between the two lines, and add that number to the calculator total.

Example: If you were born in 1963 and the present year is 1977, you would enter: **365 × 13 =**.
(Answer: 4745.)
You would then enter: **+ 4 =**.
(Answer: 4749.)

Step 2: In the list of months at left, find the month you were born in, and add the number next to it to the previous calculator total.
Continuing with the example, and imagining you were born in February, you would enter: **+ 335 =**.
(Answer: 5084.)

Step 3: Subtract the day of the month on which you were born.
Continuing with the example, and imagining you were born on February 17, you would enter: **− 17 =**.
(Answer: 5067.)

Step 1	Step 2	
1960X	January:	366
1961	February:	335
1962	March:	306
1963	April:	275
1964X	May:	245
1965	June:	214
1966	July:	184
1967	August:	153
1968X	September:	122
1969	October:	92
1970	November:	61
1971	December:	31
1972X		
1973		
1974		
1975		
1976X		
1977		
1978		
1979		
1980X		
1981		
1982		
1983		
1984X		

Step 4: If you were born in January or February of any year not marked X, subtract 1.
In the example, the month is February, and the year—1963—is not marked X, so you would enter: **− 1 =**.
(Answer: 5066.)
(If you were born in March or any later month, no matter what year it was, you would do nothing in this step. And if you were born at any time in any of the years marked X, you would also do nothing.)

Step 5: Using the new list of months at right, find the present calendar month and add the number next to it to the previous total.
In the example, if the present month were April, you would enter: **+ 91 =**.
(Answer: 5157.)

Step 6: If the current month is not January or February and the current year is not marked X, subtract 1.
In the example, the month is April (not January or February), and the year—1977—is not marked X, so you would enter: **− 1 =**.
(Answer: 5156.)
(If the month is not January or February, but the year is marked X, do not subtract 1. And if the year is not marked X, but the month is January or February, again do nothing in this step.)

Step 7: Add one number less than the day of the month it is today.
In the example, if today is April 4, you would enter: **+ 3 =**.
(Answer: 5159.)

Step 8: Multiply by 24.
In the example, you would enter: **× 24 =**.
(Answer: 123816.)

Step 9: If you do not know the time of day you were born, add 24 to the calculator total (press: **+ 24 =**), skip steps 9 and 10, and go on to step 11. Your answer will not be exact, but it will still be very close. If you do know the time, take the hour you were born and find it in the list of hours at right. Then add the number next to it to your calculator total.
In the example, if you were born at 5:36 P.M., you would ignore the 36 minutes, find 5 P.M. in the list, and enter: **+ 7 =**.
(Answer: 123823.)

Step 5	
January:	0
February:	31
March:	60
April:	91
May:	121
June:	152
July:	182
August:	213
September:	244
October:	274
November:	305
December:	335

Step 9	
Midnight:	24
1 A.M.:	23
2 A.M.:	22
3 A.M.:	21
4 A.M.:	20
5 A.M.:	19
6 A.M.:	18
7 A.M.:	17
8 A.M.:	16
9 A.M.:	15
10 A.M.:	14
11 A.M.:	13
Noon:	12
1 P.M.:	11
2 P.M.:	10
3 P.M.:	9
4 P.M.:	8
5 P.M.:	7
6 P.M.:	6
7 P.M.:	5
8 P.M.:	4
9 P.M.:	3
10 P.M.:	2
11 P.M.:	1

Step 10			
Midnight:	**0**	Noon:	**12**
1 A.M.:	**1**	1 P.M.:	**13**
2 A.M.:	**2**	2 P.M.:	**14**
3 A.M.:	**3**	3 P.M.:	**15**
4 A.M.:	**4**	4 P.M.:	**16**
5 A.M.:	**5**	5 P.M.:	**17**
6 A.M.:	**6**	6 P.M.:	**18**
7 A.M.:	**7**	7 P.M.:	**19**
8 A.M.:	**8**	8 P.M.:	**20**
9 A.M.:	**9**	9 P.M.:	**21**
10 A.M.:	**10**	10 P.M.:	**22**
11 A.M.:	**11**	11 P.M.:	**23**

Step 10: Check to see what time it is now. Again ignore the minutes. Find the hour in the new list of hours at left, and add the number given next to it to the previous calculator total.
In the example, if it is 1:20 P.M. now, you would consider it 1 P.M., and after checking the list, you would enter: **+ 13 =**.
(Answer: 123836.)

Step 11: Multiply by 60.
In the example, you would enter: **× 60 =**.
(Answer: 7430160.)

Step 12: If you do not know the minute you were born, skip steps 12 and 13, and go on to step 14. However, if you do know the minute, ignore the hour, and subtract the number of minutes from the calculator total.
In the example, since your time of birth was 5:36 P.M., you would forget about the 5, and would simply enter: **− 36 =**.
(Answer: 7430124.)

Step 13: See what time it is. Ignoring the hour, add the minutes to the calculator total.
In the example, if the time is now 1:25, you would ignore the 1, and simply enter: **+ 25 =**.
(Answer: 7430149.)

Step 14: This is your up-to-the-minute age in minutes. To figure your age in seconds, you will have to multiply by 60. But, because most calculators have only an eight-digit display space, they would register an overload at this point. You can, however, get the answer by multiplying by 6 (press: **× 6 =**), and then writing the calculator total on paper with an extra zero at the end. Or you could get the answer by multiplying it out for yourself. Either way is easy.
In the example, you would enter: **× 6 =**.
(Answer: 44580894.)
Then your age in seconds would be 445808940.

If you don't want to go through all 14 steps, you can get a rough answer in three steps:
1: Multiply your present age in years by 3156.
2. Add 263 for each month that has passed since your last birthday.
3. Write the answer down with four extra zeroes on the end.
You can also use this method to check the answer you arrived at using all 14 steps. The two answers should be less than 1,500,000 seconds apart (a half of a month in seconds).
How close was your guess to the actual answer?

UPS AND DOWNS

How long do you think it would take you to get from any number in the world to 1 **if** you had to keep multiplying and dividing to get there? Here's a solitaire game that will give you the answer. It may surprise you. To play, pick any number with less than six digits, and enter it on your calculator. (It is best to pick a fairly small number to begin with, and go on to larger ones later.)

If the number you picked is odd, multiply it by 3 and add 1. (Enter: **× 3 + 1 =**). If it is even, divide it by 2 (enter: **÷ 2 =**).

Do the same with the answer, and continue in this way with all future answers.

The number on the display will go up and down, but eventually, no matter what number you started from, you will reach 1. Here's an example, using 53 as the starting number:

53 odd (× 3 + 1 =)
160 even (÷ 2 =)
80 even (÷ 2 =)
40 even (÷ 2 =)
20 even (÷ 2 =)
10 even (÷ 2 =)
5 odd (× 3 + 1 =)
16 even (÷ 2 =)
8 even (÷ 2 =)
4 even (÷ 2 =)
2 even (÷ 2 =)
1

Some numbers will come down to 1 rapidly. It took 11 steps to go from 53 to 1. The size of the original number is sometimes a clue to how long it will take, but not always. Try a little number like 7. Then try 16384, and be surprised. A few small numbers, like 27, 31, and 41, are very stubborn indeed. Each of them takes over 100 steps and reaches as high as 9232 along the way.

NUMBER TREES

Have you ever heard the old saying, "Money doesn't grow on trees"? Well, it may be true of money, but here are some trees with **numbers** growing on them. In fact, together the two trees contain every number from 1 to 162. Every branch is exactly where it must be for the trees to grow properly according to a definite rule. Your task is to figure out what that rule is. Once you do, you will be able to place the next branch, number 163, in its proper position.

This is a pretty tricky puzzle. To solve it, start with a small section of the tree, and see how one branch might have grown from the one next to it. For example, in the area shaded in yellow, the numbers 7 and 70 both grow out of number 49. Ask yourself and your calculator what calculation can be made with both 7 and 70 that would produce an answer of 49. When you think you know, test your answer on other parts of the trees. For example, ask yourself if the same rule could be used with both 49 and 94 to produce 97. When you are sure you know, apply this rule to the number 163, and find the place where it fits into the tree.

The answer is given on the next page, along with some other puzzles and games you can play with the trees.

This is the rule that makes the trees grow: To add a new number, multiply each digit in the number by itself, and add up the results. Then find that number on the trees and attach the new branch to it. So to place number 163 correctly, you would have had to enter:

1 × 1 = (1)   **6 × 6 = (36)**   **3 × 3 = (9)**
and: **1 + 36 + 9 = (46)**

Then you would have had to look for number 46 on the trees and attach 163 to it, as shown in green in the drawing at left.

Now that you know what the trees stand for, you can use them for several number games. For one thing, there is no number that could not find a place on these trees. You can entertain yourself endlessly by dreaming up numbers and then testing them to see where they fit. For example, take a very large number like 897,412,266. Following the rule, you would enter:

8 × 8 = (64)   **9 × 9 = (81)**   **7 × 7 = (49)**
4 × 4 = (16)   **1 × 1 = (1)**   **2 × 2 = (4)**
2 × 2 = (4)   **6 × 6 = (36)**   **6 × 6 = (36)**

and: **64 + 81 + 49 + 16 + 1 + 4 + 4 + 36 + 36 = (291)**.

Now, do the same with 291:
2 × 2 = (4)   **9 × 9 = (81)**   **1 × 1 = (1)**
and: **4 + 81 + 1 = (86)**.

So you would then place 291 on the smaller tree as a branch of 86, and 897,412,266 would be a branch of 291.

Because the trees look so nice, you might even want to make a large drawing of them to hang on a wall and then add a few numbers every day. People will wonder what the numbers mean, and when they ask, invite them to solve the puzzle as you did.
You can keep the tree growing by dreaming up new numbers like 897,412,266 and adding them on. Or you can just keep adding numbers from 163 on up. Either way, you will find that though you know what number you are adding, where it ends up on the tree will always be a surprise. As you keep adding numbers, you will notice some very strange things about the trees. The two trees never meet but always remain separate; one tree grows much faster than the other; and when you arrive at the bottom of the small tree, you stop there forever, because 1 × 1 = 1. But when you get to the bottom of the large tree, you can go back up into the tree because 4 × 4 = 16, and 16 is already high up on a branch.

CAT AND MICE

You can also use the number trees as a playing board for a game of Cat and Mice.

This is a game for two or more players, the more the better. Also needed are as many markers as there are players, a set of dice, and a calculator.

To start, each player produces a random number on the calculator by dividing an eight-digit number by another eight-digit number, without looking at the keys he is pressing. As each player does this, write down the second digit from the left in the answer. Whoever has the highest number is the cat; the others are mice. The mouse with the second-highest number goes first, the next highest goes second, and so on. In the case of ties, use the dice to determine who goes first.

The Cat

The cat places his marker on any number he wishes. The mice then place their markers on any number they choose, but they try to keep as far away from the cat as possible. The cat moves first by producing another random number. He again uses only the second digit from the left and moves his marker exactly that number of spaces to try to catch a mouse. If he lands on the same circle as a mouse, he has caught the mouse, and that player removes his marker and leaves the game. If he passes over a mouse, that mouse is safe. The cat may not change directions while counting off a move, except when he comes to a dead-end branch.

The Mice

After the cat has moved, each of the mice move in turn, using the same method the cat does. But a mouse may change direction in counting off his move. And if he comes to a dead-end branch (such as the number 88 in the upper left-hand corner of the large tree), after calling "mousehole," he may continue his move from the number that is one more or one less than that number. (In the case of 88, he could jump to 87 or 89 all the way on the other side of the board.) Once a mouse jumps, he cannot jump from the mousehole he landed in. The only jump that the cat can make is from 1 to 4 and back. Mice may occupy a number together, but if the cat lands on it, all are caught.

Game Tips

All players must move within five seconds after their number comes up on the calculator, and once they start counting off a move they may not change their mind and take it back. The game ends when the cat has caught all the mice . . . or gets tired of chasing them.

A STITCH IN TIME SAVES NINE

As you may already know, 9 is an odd number. In fact, sometimes it's positively weird. Perhaps its odd behavior is all chance. Or maybe there actually is something special about it. Why else would people say things like, "Cats have nine lives" or "A stitch in time saves nine"? Try these amazing calculator tricks based on the number 9, and judge for yourself.

You don't have to go very far to make strange things happen with 9. For example, your calculator will begin to stutter as soon as you try some simple division problems. Press **1 ÷ 9 =**, **2 ÷ 9 =, 3 ÷ 9 =,** and so on. Even more interesting things happen when you start with numbers like 10, 20, 30, or others ending in 0, and then divide by 9. There are some exceptions to all this repetition, however. As you may have already discovered, dividing 9 into an even multiple of 9 (such as 9, 18, or 27) will give your calculator a chance to catch its breath.

Want more proof that 9 is special? Pick any number that does **not** read the same backwards and forwards. (That is, don't pick a number like 7002007, 8118, or 6. The reason will soon be obvious.) Write your number down so you don't forget it, and enter it on the calculator. Press the minus key and enter the same number again but **backwards**. Finally, press the equals key.

Example: 874326 − 623478 = 250848

Write down the answer and clear the calculator. Then add up all the digits the answer contains. (In this example, you would press **2 + 5 + 0 + 8 + 4 + 8 = 27.**) If the new answer contains more than one digit, clear the calculator and add the individual digits again.
(Here you would press **2 + 7 = 9.**)
The sum of the digits will always come out to 9!

If that isn't enough, take the first answer and **add** it to itself backwards. The total of the digits will again equal 9.

Example: 250848 + 848052 = 1098900
1 + 0 + 9 + 8 + 9 + 0 + 0 = 27
2 + 7 = 9

In fact, if you continue calculating in this way, whether you add or subtract, you will always get a number whose digits add up to 9. Just remember to clear the calculator between steps.

The example continues:
1098900 + 0098901 = 1197801
1 + 1 + 9 + 7 + 8 + 0 + 1 = 27
2 + 7 = 9
or **1098900 − 0098901 = 999999**
9 + 9 + 9 + 9 + 9 + 9 = 54
5 + 4 = 9

The answer to the subtraction is especially dazzling. Of course, a row of 9s will not always be the end result. But one thing is for sure: When you subtract, you will always eventually reach a number that reads the same backwards and forwards, as this one does. Once that happens you can't go any further with the subtractions, because the result would be 0. (This was the reason certain numbers had to be ruled out at the beginning.) But you can continue with the **additions** for as long as you like—or at least until your calculator

overloads. The best way to carry this trick out for a long time is to alternate between adding and subtracting. When you do that, if you happen to subtract a large number from a small one and get an answer below zero (a negative number, marked on the display by a minus sign), the Rule of Nines will still hold true and you can continue adding and subtracting as usual.

You can use this trick to amaze people by seeming to guess their age—with, of all things, the help of their telephone number. If they are less than 10 years old it is very simple; if older, only a little harder. To begin with, let's assume the person is under 10. Tell him to enter his age and press the plus sign on the calculator.

Example: 8 +

Now for the hocus-pocus. Tell him to enter his telephone number and press the minus key. (If there are letters or dashes in the phone number, tell him to ignore them.)

The example continues:
7444950 −

Then tell him to enter his phone number backwards and press the equals sign.

The example continues: 0594447 =

Now ask him to let you see the answer.

In the example: All you would see is the answer 6850511. Of course, the telephone number was just a smoke screen. You know, but your victim doesn't, that the phone number and the reversed subtraction will all boil away and what is left over will be his age.

> **Important:** For this trick, be sure the answer is above zero; if there is a minus sign in the display, add enough nines to force the number to rise above zero. For example, if the number is −5499991 (seven digits), add 9999999 (seven 9s), and a new number will appear without the minus sign. In this case the new number will be 4500008. Now write down the number, clear the calculator and add up the digits in the answer.

The example continues:
6 + 8 + 5 + 0 + 5 + 1 + 1 = 26
2 + 6 = 8.
The answer is the age.

Since the answer will always be a single digit, you may wonder how this trick can work for anyone over 9 years old. The solution is simple: Once a person passes 9, you mentally add 9 to the number on the calculator. This means that the number that will show on the display for a 10-year-old is 1, for an 11-year-old is 2, for a 12-year-old is 3, and so on. So if you get a number which could not possibly be the person's age, just keep adding 9 to it until the number seems about right for that person. The chances are very good that this will be his age. It gets a little risky only if you have no idea how old the person is.

For example, if your victim is of high-school age and his number comes out to be 7, add 9 and you get 16. That must be his age, because if you add 9 again, you get 25, and that's too old. On the other hand, if you're trying this trick on your great-grandmother, who you guess is about 80, and her number is 7, again keep adding nines until you come to a number around 80. In this case, it will be 79 (7 + eight 9s).

Here is another trick you can do to reduce any number to 9. Pick any number above 9.

Example: 88437192
Find the sum of its digits. Do this in your head or with pencil and paper, so you don't lose track of the original number.

The example continues:
8 + 8 + 4 + 3 + 7 + 1 + 9 + 2 = 42
Subtract this total from the original number.

The example continues:
88437192 − 42 = 88437150
If the answer is greater than 9, divide by 9.

The example continues:
88437150 ÷ 9 = 9826350
Again, find the sum of the digits, subtract, and divide by 9.

The example continues:
9 + 8 + 2 + 6 + 3 + 5 + 0 = 33
9826350 − 33 = 9826317 ÷ 9 = 1091813

Keep adding, subtracting, and dividing in this way, and—you guessed it—you will eventually reach 9. It never fails.

The example continues:
1 + 0 + 9 + 1 + 8 + 1 + 3 = 23
and **1091813 − 23 = 1091790 ÷ 9 = 121310**
1 + 2 + 1 + 3 + 1 + 0 = 8
and **121310 − 8 = 121302 ÷ 9 = 13478**
1 + 3 + 4 + 7 + 8 = 23
and **13478 − 23 = 13455 ÷ 9 = 1495**
1 + 4 + 9 + 5 = 19
and **1495 − 19 = 1476 ÷ 9 = 164**
1 + 6 + 4 = 11 and **164 − 11 = 153 ÷ 9 = 17**
1 + 7 = 8 and **17 − 8 = 9!**

Just in case you are not convinced that 9 is a pretty strange number, here is one last demonstration. Pick any 2-digit number and write it down.

Example: 38
Now, using your calculator, subtract the smaller digit from the larger.
Example: 8 − 3 = 5
Multiply the difference by 9.
Example: 5 × 9 = 45
Now, if the first digit of the number you wrote down was smaller than the second digit, add the whole original number to the calculator total, and you will have the reverse of your original number!
Example: 45 + 38 = 83.
But if the first digit of the number you wrote down was larger than the second digit, clear the calculator and subtract the calculator total from the original number. You will again have the reverse.
New example:
Original number: **97**
$$9 - 7 = 2$$
$$2 \times 9 = 18$$
$$\text{and } 97 - 18 = 79$$

SEVEN COME 11 OR MAYBE 13

$123123 \div 7 = 17589$
$\div 11 = 1599 \div 13 = 123$

You can bamboozle your friends with this trick, but first try it on yourself for practice. Pick any three-digit number, from 100 to 999, and enter it twice to produce a six-digit number. For example: press **123**, then press **123** again. The display will read: **123123.**

Then divide by 7, divide again by 11, and divide a third time by 13. The final answer will **always** be the same as your original three-digit number! Try a few other numbers just to be convinced. It's pretty amazing, until you figure out the secret.

The secret: If you enter any three-digit number twice in a row, what you are actually doing to it is multiplying it by 1001. Press **123 × 1001 =** to see that this is so. And if you divide any number by 7, 11, and 13, all you are really doing is dividing it by 1001. This is so because $7 \times 11 \times 13 = 1001$. So all you have done in the trick is to multiply and divide by the same number.

You can do some other number magic with the same trick. Tell a friend you will give him a lucky number, as a favor of course. Tell him to enter any three-digit number twice, as described above, and to divide by 11, divide again by 13, and divide a third time by the original three-digit number. The answer will **always** be 7, as you may already have guessed.

Try the same thing, announcing that you will produce an unlucky number. In this case, tell your friend to divide the six-digit number by 7,

11, and the original three-digit number. The answer will of course be 13.

If you happen to know someone who is 7 or 13 years old, all the better, because you can tell him that his answer will be equal to his age. (Likewise, you can tell anyone who is 11 years old to divide the six-digit number by 7, 13, and the original three-digit number, and he will get an answer of 11.) Of course, you can easily modify these tricks to suit other ages. For example, if you're using this on a person who is 14, bring his answer down to 7 and tell him to double it; or down to 11 and tell him to add 3.

There is a similar trick you can do with four-digit numbers. Repeating a four-digit number to produce an eight-digit number is the same as multiplying by 10,001. And because it just so happens that 73×137 also equals 10,001, you can probably already guess how the trick will work. Just as you divide the six-digit number by 7, 11, and 13 to reduce it back to the three-digit number, you can divide the eight-digit version for "guessing" ages.

Simply figure out in advance the number you need to subtract from 73 or 137 to reach the person's age, and the rest is easy. All these tricks are most effective if you perform them with great ceremony and all sorts of hocus-pocus. Insist that your victim not let you see the numbers he has pressed, and act pleased and a little surprised when the correct answer miraculously appears on the calculator.

TRUCK DRIVER

This is a game for two or more players, each with a calculator. You will also need the gameboard here, a playing piece, and markers (small enough to fit the squares on the board) for each player. You can use dressmaker pins with colored heads, if you don't mind making tiny holes in the book pages, or cut many little squares out of construction paper. The two players should use different colors, and each player should use only one color.

The object of the game is to accumulate the highest point total while "delivering freight" to the towns shown on the distance chart.

About the gameboard:

The Truckdriver gameboard is in the form of a distance chart. Charts of this type are often given on highway maps to make it easy to figure out how far it is from one town to another. A truck-driver who wants to go from Niceville to Weeping Water, for example, would look for Niceville in the alphabetical list of towns at the left and for Weeping Water in the list at the top. He would then follow the horizontal row of numbers across the page from Niceville and the vertical column of figures down the page from Weeping Water as far as the box where the two lines cross. The number that appears in that box is the driving distance between the two towns. In the example, it is 60 leagues. In real life, of course, the distance would be given in kilometers or miles, depending on where you live. Incidentally, all the names on the chart are taken from real places. You may recognize some of them as places you know. But the distances are imaginary.

	Apple Pie Hill	Birdman	Birdsnest	Bivalve	Blue Bell	Braggadocio	Buckshutem	Cando	Cheesequake	Clover Lick	Cocoa Beach
Apple Pie Hill		23	11	23	40	22	7	47	8	1	4
Birdman	23		22	5	51	36	29	49	15	23	18
Birdsnest	11	22		24	51	13	12	55	16	12	14
Bivalve	23	5	24		50	40	30	45	16	24	19
Blue Bell	40	51	51	50		61	46	19	38	40	40
Braggadocio	22	36	13	40	61		15	65	29	21	26
Buckshutem	7	29	12	30	46	15		50	14	6	11
Cando	47	49	55	45	19	65	50		10	11	11
Cheesequake	8	15	16	16	38	29	14	10		8	4
Clover Lick	1	23	12	24	40	21	6	11	8		5
Cocoa Beach	4	18	14	19	40	26	11	11	4	5	
Cornstalk	39	27	49	22	39	61	46	31	31	40	35
Dreahook	46	47	57	43	23	66	51	34	39	45	41
Eek	24	30	34	27	22	44	29	11	19	23	23
Egg Harbor	15	14	24	12	37	37	22	10	7	16	11
Enigma	8	20	19	19	34	28	13	5	5	7	5
Evening Shade	10	24	3	27	50	13	10	22	16	11	12
Foloom	61	68	72	65	21	82	67	49	59	61	61
Goodnews Bay	42	27	48	22	47	64	49	36	35	43	38
Jackpot	10	17	19	16	35	31	17	6	4	10	6
Little Ferry	26	27	37	24	26	49	34	17	20	27	22
Londonbridge	8	26	19	24	35	26	11	7	11	8	8
Loveladies	28	17	36	13	40	50	35	21	21	29	24
Meddybemps	79	73	90	69	54	102	87	70	73	81	75
Muleshoe	11	14	20	12	38	33	18	10	4	12	7
Mystic Islands	24	12	32	8	42	45	30	18	17	24	20
Niceville	75	60	81	55	74	97	82	69	68	76	71
Picayune	15	26	26	25	25	35	21	3	13	14	15
Plumbsock	20	41	19	43	49	11	13	28	27	19	24
Pretty Prairie	17	8	21	6	43	39	24	15	10	18	13
Quoddy Head	35	16	38	12	54	51	42	31	27	35	31
Raisin	16	29	6	32	56	7	15	28	22	17	19
Shiner	28	34	39	30	19	48	33	16	23	27	25
Ship Bottom	14	26	3	29	54	10	12	25	19	14	16
Sleepy Hollow	67	60	78	55	50	89	75	57	61	68	63
Soda Springs	4	23	8	25	44	20	7	15	9	4	6
Sopchoppy	81	88	94	85	42	103	88	70	80	82	82
Weeping Water	18	19	27	16	33	39	27	10	11	18	14
Wink	85	84	96	80	54	105	91	73	80	84	82
Zap	81	92	92	86	40	101	86	69	79	80	81
Zarephath	71	82	82	76	31	92	77	59	69	71	71

Cornstalk	Dreahook	Eek	Egg Harbor	Enigma	Evening Shade	Foloom	Goodnews Bay	Jackpot	Little Ferry	Londonbridge	Loveladies	Meddybemps	Muleshoe	Mystic Islands	Niceville	Picayune	Plumbsock	Pretty Prairie	Quoddy Head	Raisin	Shiner	Ship Bottom	Sleepy Hollow	Soda Springs	Sopchoppy	Weeping Water	Wink	Zap	Zarephath
39	46	24	15	8	10	61	42	10	26	8	28	79	11	24	75	15	20	17	35	16	28	14	67	4	81	18	85	81	71
27	47	30	14	20	24	68	27	17	27	26	17	73	14	12	60	26	41	8	16	29	34	26	60	23	88	19	84	92	82
49	57	34	24	19	3	72	48	19	37	19	36	90	20	32	81	26	19	21	38	6	39	3	78	8	94	27	96	92	82
22	43	27	12	19	27	65	22	16	24	24	13	69	12	8	55	25	43	6	12	32	30	29	55	25	85	16	80	86	76
39	23	22	37	34	50	21	47	35	26	35	40	54	38	42	74	25	49	43	54	56	19	54	50	44	42	33	54	40	31
61	66	44	37	28	13	82	64	31	49	26	50	102	33	45	97	35	11	39	51	7	48	10	89	20	103	39	105	101	92
46	51	29	22	13	10	67	49	17	34	11	35	87	18	30	82	21	13	24	42	15	33	12	75	7	88	27	91	86	77
31	34	11	10	5	22	49	36	6	17	7	21	70	10	18	69	3	28	15	31	28	16	25	57	15	70	10	73	68	59
31	39	19	7	5	16	59	35	4	20	11	21	73	4	17	68	13	27	10	27	22	23	19	61	9	80	11	80	79	69
40	45	23	16	7	11	61	43	10	27	8	29	81	12	24	76	14	19	18	35	17	27	14	68	4	82	18	84	80	71
35	41	23	11	5	12	61	38	6	22	8	24	75	7	20	71	15	13	31	19	25	16	63	6	82	14	82	81	71	
	26	23	24	33	47	52	8	29	17	38	11	47	28	15	38	34	59	23	17	54	22	51	34	41	68	22	60	70	63
26		23	34	39	56	26	34	35	20	41	32	38	37	35	58	35	62	39	43	62	18	59	27	49	43	29	42	45	37
23	23		15	5	16	58	45	9	25	3	30	78	13	24	78	12	19	19	36	22	25	20	66	10	80	18	82	78	68
24	34	15		9	23	59	28	6	14	14	14	68	4	9	61	12	35	5	21	30	21	27	55	17	76	6	77	79	69
33	39	5	9		18	55	37	4	20	4	23	73	7	18	70	9	24	13	31	24	21	21	60	11	76	12	78	75	65
47	56	16	23	18		71	49	18	34	18	36	91	19	32	82	25	19	25	39	6	38	4	79	7	92	26	94	91	81
52	26	58	59	55	71		60	55	42	56	56	41	59	57	86	46	70	60	69	77	35	75	38	65	22	50	38	20	11
8	34	45	28	37	49	60		33	25	42	15	52	31	19	33	39	62	26	12	55	30	52	39	44	74	26	65	77	71
29	35	9	6	4	18	55	33		5	19	12	58	13	11	57	16	40	14	24	37	12	34	46	24	66	4	67	67	58
17	20	25	14	20	34	42	25	5		23	14	53	17	15	55	19	44	18	27	44	7	38	41	31	62	8	62	62	53
38	41	3	14	4	18	56	42	19	23		28	76	12	23	74	10	22	18	35	24	23	22	64	12	78	16	80	76	66
11	32	30	14	23	36	56	15	12	14	28		57	17	5	48	24	48	12	14	43	20	40	44	30	74	12	68	76	66
47	38	78	68	73	91	41	52	58	53	76	57		70	61	67	73	97	69	63	97	55	91	13	84	32	62	13	38	41
28	37	13	4	7	19	59	31	13	17	12	17	70		13	64	13	31	6	24	26	23	23	59	13	80	9	80	79	69
15	35	24	9	18	32	57	19	11	15	23	5	61	13		52	31	43	7	13	38	22	35	49	25	77	10	72	78	68
38	58	78	61	70	82	86	33	57	55	74	48	67	64	52		72	95	59	45	87	60	84	54	77	96	60	81	98	94
34	35	12	12	9	25	46	39	16	19	10	24	73	13	31	72		42	29	42	42	12	39	54	29	56	18	67	55	45
59	62	19	35	24	19	70	62	40	44	22	48	97	31	43	95	42		37	55	13	44	16	85	20	92	37	101	90	80
23	39	19	5	13	25	60	26	14	18	18	12	69	6	7	59	29	37		18	32	25	29	58	19	80	10	80	84	74
17	43	36	21	31	39	69	12	24	27	35	14	63	24	13	45	42	55	18		44	34	41	50	36	85	23	77	87	80
54	62	22	30	24	6	77	55	37	44	24	43	97	26	38	87	42	13	32	44		44	3	83	13	98	76	91	97	87
22	18	25	21	21	38	35	30	12	7	23	20	55	23	22	60	12	44	25	34	44		30	53	20	67	6	69	69	59
51	59	20	27	21	4	75	52	34	38	22	40	91	23	35	84	39	16	29	41	3	30		82	10	96	30	98	94	84
34	27	66	55	60	79	38	39	46	41	64	44	13	59	49	54	54	85	58	50	83	53	82		41	45	27	54	44	34
41	49	10	17	11	7	65	44	24	31	12	30	84	13	25	77	29	20	19	36	13	20	10	41		86	20	88	84	74
68	43	80	76	76	92	22	74	66	62	78	74	32	80	77	96	56	92	80	85	98	67	96	45	86		70	22	6	12
22	29	18	6	12	26	50	26	4	8	16	12	62	9	10	60	18	37	10	23	76	6	30	27	20	70		25	29	24
60	42	82	77	78	94	38	65	67	62	80	68	13	80	72	81	67	101	80	77	91	69	98	54	88	22	25		28	31
70	45	78	79	75	91	20	77	67	62	76	76	38	79	78	98	55	90	84	87	97	69	94	44	84	6	29	28		10
63	37	68	69	65	81	11	71	58	53	66	66	41	69	68	94	45	80	74	80	87	59	84	34	74	12	24	31	10	

The game is played like this:

1. Each player places his marker on any **numbered** square he wishes. More than one player may start from the same square and may land on the same square at any time during the game.

Example:
Benny (playing as Red) puts his playing piece on Apple Pie Hill-Birdman (23).

Dexter (playing as Blue) puts his playing piece on Birdsnest-Bivalve (24).

	Apple Pie Hill	Birdman	Birdsnest	Bivalve	Blue Bell	Braggadocio	Buckshutem
Apple Pie Hill		23	11	23	40	22	7
Birdman	23		22	5	51	36	29
Birdsnest	11	22		24	51	13	12
Bivalve	23	5	24		50	40	30
Blue Bell	40	51	51	50		61	46
Braggadocio	22	36	13	40	61		15
Buckshutem	7	29	12	30	46	15	

In naming the squares, the town on the left-hand side is given first and the one at the top second. In following the examples, be sure you don't get them mixed up. Apple Pie Hill-Birdman is a different square from Birdman-Apple Pie Hill.

2. Toss a coin, roll dice, or cut cards to determine the order of the players.

In the sample game here, Benny goes first.

3. The players take turns, and each player does three things in each turn.

a. He enters the number of his square on his calculator.

Example:
Benny is on a square numbered 23, so he enters **23** on his calculator.

b. He puts his markers at the ends of the two rows that meet on his square. Once a circle has been covered with a marker, it cannot be covered again.

	Apple Pie Hill	Birdman	Birdsnest	Bivalve	Blue Bell	Braggadocio	Buckshutem
Apple Pie Hill		23	11	23	40	22	7
Birdman	23		22	5	51	36	29
Birdsnest	11	22		24	51	13	12
Bivalve	23	5	24		50	40	30
Blue Bell	40	51	51	50		61	46
Braggadocio	22	36	13	40	61		15
Buckshutem	7	29	12	30	46	15	

Example:
Benny has put his markers on circles for Apple Pie Hill at left and Birdman at the top.

c. He reads the last digit on his calculator display and moves his playing piece **horizontally or vertically** exactly that number of squares in any direction he chooses. If the last digit is zero, he uses the next-to-the-last to move. Changing directions while counting off a move is not allowed. Empty squares count in moving the markers, but no one may land on one. So, if you want to move horizontally, but that would land you on an empty square, you must move vertically.

Example:
Benny reads the last digit on his calculator display. It is the 3 in the number 23. Therefore he may move three squares in any direction. He decides to move to the right, and he lands on Apple Pie Hill—Blue Bell (40).

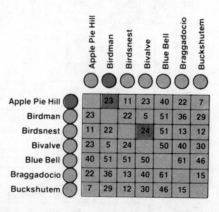

That is the end of his turn.

Now, Dexter does the same three things. He enters his number (**24**) on the calculator.

He puts his markers on the right circles.

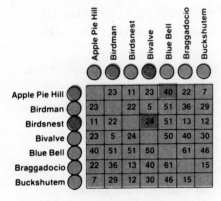

He moves his playing piece four spaces, to Buckshutem-Bivalve (**30**).

That is the end of his turn.

4. On later turns, the players continue to do the same things, **adding** the number in the new square to the previous calculator total.

Example:
Benny **adds** the number on his new square to his calculator total by pressing **+ 40 =**. His calculator display then looks like this:

He covers any circles at the ends of the rows that are still blank, in this case, only Blue Bell at the top, since he had already covered Apple Pie Hill.

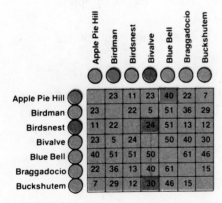

He then moves three spaces, because 3 is still his last digit.

5. Play ends when all the circles are covered. At that point, the markers on the circles at the top are compared to those on the circles at the side. If a player has covered both circles for any one town, he may then put his marker on the box located where that town's rows cross, in the empty diagonal on the playing board.

Example:
At the end of play, the board might look like this:

	Apple Pie Hill	Birdman	Birdsnest	Bivalve	Blue Bell	Braggadocio	Buckshutem
Apple Pie Hill		23	11	23	40	22	7
Birdman	23		22	5	51	36	29
Birdsnest	11	22		24	51	13	12
Bivalve	23	5	24		50	40	30
Blue Bell	40	51	51	50		61	46
Braggadocio	22	36	13	40	61		15
Buckshutem	7	29	12	30	46	15	

Each player adds 25 bonus points to the total on his calculator for each circle he has covered, and 50 extra points for each box. The one with the highest score wins.

For the section of the board pictured, both players have seven circles covered, for a total of 175 bonus points each (7 × 25 = 175). In addition they each have two boxes to their name, for a total of 100 extra points each (2 × 50 = 100).

POKULATOR

Poker anyone? Whether or not you know this popular card game, you can play an easy, fast-moving variation on your calculator. Pokulator is a game for two or more players. Each player must have an individual calculator. If you play the betting version, you will also need 50 poker chips (or other counters) for each player.

Simple pokulator

1. Each player produces a surprise, or random, number on his calculator. To do this, press an eight-digit number without looking at the keys, and then **divide** it by another eight-digit number produced in the same way.

2. Your hand contains five "cards" as in regular poker. They are the last five digits on the right side of the display. For example, if you pressed: **64949455 ÷ 75524711 =**, your calculator would read: **0.8599762**, and your hand would then be: **99762** as shown at left. The surprise number almost never has fewer than five digits; but if that should happen, start over.

3. In simple pokulator, the players show their hands to each other as soon as their surprise numbers come up. The player with the highest hand, according to the following list, wins—and scores one point. The first to reach 10 points wins the match.

0.85 99762

How to rate the hands

Highest: Five of a kind. All numbers the same. Example: 33333.

Second highest: Four of a kind. Four numbers the same. Example: 82888. (The order of the numbers is unimportant. You can rearrange them mentally if you wish.)

Third highest: Straight flush. Five different odd numbers or five different even numbers. Examples: 31957 (13579), or 48062 (02468). Zero counts as an even number.

Fourth highest: Full house. Three of one number and two of another. Example: 76676 (777 66).

Fifth highest: Straight. Five numbers in a row. Example 68475 (45678). In pokulator, there is no number, like the ace in a deck of cards, that can be either high or low. Naturally, the highest number is 9 and the lowest is 0. But straights can start and end anywhere. This means that 67890 and 89012 are acceptable as straights.

Sixth highest: Three of a kind. Three numbers the same. Example: 46445.

Seventh highest: Flush. Five odd numbers or five even numbers. Example: 11597.

Eighth highest: Two pairs. Two of one number and two of another. Example: 91419 (99 11 4).

Ninth highest: One pair. Two of one number. Example: 37647.

Tenth highest: High card. If no better hand is shown, the player with the highest single number wins. Example 47982 beats 61783, because 9 is higher than 8.

As you may know, the order of the hands is not exactly the same as in regular poker. In actual play, the five highest hands are extremely rare, and a simple pair (ninth highest) is often enough to win. If two players are tied with the same kind of hand, the one with the highest cards wins. For example, 77777 beats 44444 because 7 is higher than 4; and 13579 (straight flush) beats 02468 (also a straight flush) because 9 is higher than 8. But note that 77722 (full house) is better than 66688 (also a full house) because the three 7s are higher than the three 6s, and that is the part of the hand that counts most. It does not matter in this case that the 8 is higher than the 7 and the 2. If high cards are also tied, the winner is determined by the next highest card. Thus 77744 beats 77722, and 38190 beats 96751. If the winning hands are identical, the players who are tied play a new hand to break the tie. Finally, if a hand fits two of the ten categories, it is rated as the higher one. Example: 91519 is two pairs (eighth highest), but it is also a flush (seventh highest) and is rated as a flush.

Betting pokulator

The betting version of pokulator is much the same as the simple version—except that instead of comparing hands right away, the players hold their calculators like card hands, so the others can't see their numbers, and they bet against each other with poker chips.

1. Everyone sits around a table or in a circle. Each player starts with 50 chips. At the beginning of every hand, before the players even get their numbers, each player puts one chip in the center, or "pot." This is called anteing, and it is done so everyone has an equal stake in the game.

2. The betting begins for real after everyone has gotten his surprise number. On the first hand, the youngest player may begin the betting. In later hands, the winner of the previous hand goes first. The betting always moves clockwise (from right to left) around the circle, and everyone must bet in his proper turn. Depending on how good his hand is, the first player may make a bet or not make a bet (pass). If he passes, the next player in turn can also pass or he can make a bet. When a player decides to bet, he places from one to five

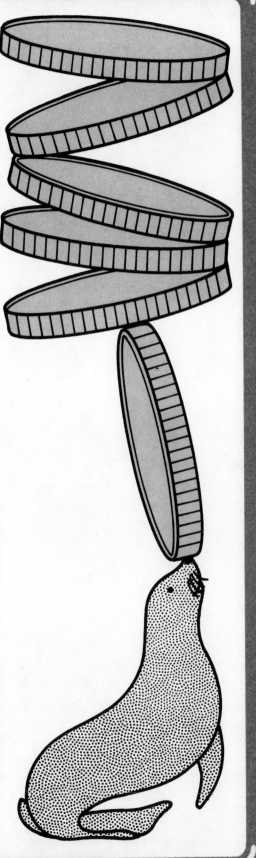

chips in the pot and announces the number he has bet. (Five chips is the maximum bet allowed.) After the first bet is made, each player, going in turn, must then decide to do one of three things:

a. If he thinks his hand is too poor to win, he may **leave the game** for the present hand rather than lose any more chips. This is often the wisest thing to do. He puts no chips in the pot, and he places his calculator face down on the table. He can no longer win the pot, even if his hand later turns out to be highest.

b. If he thinks his hand may win, he **matches** the bet by placing the same number of chips in the pot, and he stays in the running.

c. If he thinks his hand is very strong, he can **raise** the original bet by first **matching** it and then **adding** from one to five extra chips to the pot.

> **Bluffing:** It is not always necessary to have a good hand to win. Betting **as if** you had a good hand may frighten the others out of the game. (It can also lose you a lot of chips if they stay.) If everyone leaves the game, the last one to bet wins the pot no matter what his hand is. He does not even have to show it to the others.

If a bet is raised, all the players must match the full amount of the raise, or else leave the game. There is a limit of three raises for each round of betting. No one may raise his own bet—only another player's. The betting ends when no new raises are announced or when the third raise is matched by all the players. At that point, everyone shows his display, with the last person to bet going first. The person with the highest hand wins, provided he has stayed in the game to the end. A player who has run out of chips in the middle of a hand may play until the end of that hand without matching bets (though he may not make bets of his own). If he wins the hand, he will then have new chips to play with and may stay in the game. If he loses, he is out of the game for good. Play continues until one person has won all the chips.

Draw pokulator

For all the fun of real poker, try this variation in which everyone has a chance to improve his hand after the first round of betting. Instead of comparing hands after the betting round already described, each player who wants to may discard from one to three of his numbers and replace them with new ones. This is how you do it:

Give each player a sheet of paper and a pencil, and explain that each of the five digits in each hand is represented by a letter. The first digit on the left is "A," the second digit "B," the third "C," the fourth "D," and the fifth, on the far right, "E," as shown below.

9 9 7 6 2
A B C D E

In this hand, the two 9s (A and B) are worth keeping. The 7, 6, and 2 (C, D, and E) do not contribute anything to the hand, so they would probably be discarded. To discard numbers, each player writes the letters for the numbers he is getting rid of—not the numbers themselves—on a sheet of paper. Everyone writes his letters (or "NONE") at the same time. The player with the hand shown above would write "CDE" to discard 762. Then each person passes his paper to the player on his left and announces how many

cards he is exchanging. The players who receive the lettered papers write any number they wish (from 0 to 9) above each of the letters. Let us imagine that the player who received the paper in the example wrote 369 above the CDE. When the new numbers are filled in, the papers are returned to their owners. The new numbers are substituted for the old ones, mentally or on paper, and in that way a new hand is produced. After the substitutions are made, the sample hand would be:

9 9 3 6 9
A B C D E

The pair of 9s have improved to three of a kind! A new round of betting begins, based on the new hands. The betting starts with the person who bet last in the previous round. The rules are the same, and bets are added to the existing pot. When the betting is finished, everyone shows their hands, and the winner takes the pot.

GROWN-UPS

This is a game for two or more players. It is best if each player has his own calculator. If not, use paper and pencil to keep score. You will also need a pair of dice, the gameboard on pages 44 and 45, one marker for each player, an elastic band for each marker. The object of the game is to get a score 1000 or more points higher than the scores of the other players.

Playing the game:

1. Each player enters **1000** on his calculator and places his marker on **START** (square 1).

2. Dice are rolled to determine the order of the players. High roll goes first.

3. When the order is established, each player in turn rolls the dice and advances his marker across the playing board the number of squares the dice indicate. He then follows the instructions given on the square where he lands. These usually involve a calculation. Unless he has rolled a double (two dice with the same number), his turn ends. A double wins him an extra turn, which he takes immediately.

4. In counting off moves, players must follow the number sequence shown on the gameboard, except where the directions say otherwise.

5. The most important square is **START** because the first player to go around the board and reach or pass **START** adds a large bonus to his score. Whenever this happens, all the other players return to **START** without receiving a bonus, and play continues from there in the usual order.

6. When any player's score falls below zero or trails the leader's score by 1000 points or more, that player must leave the game.

7. If any instruction cannot possibly be followed, it should be ignored.

8. When you land on a starred square (*), see the rules shown opposite for additional information. In a short time you'll remember them, but for now, simply pick up the playing pieces (noting where they go) and flip the page back. Once you've read the rule, flip the page again and resume the game.

Square 3: Subtract your age in years as of your last birthday. If you land on this square, you are automatically insured until someone reaches **START**. This will be important if you land on squares 62, 63, or 64. Place an elastic band around your marker as a reminder.

Square 5: It's fine if the answer contains a decimal. Let it be.

Squares 8, 9, 22, 23, 36, 37, 50, and 51: If you are on any of these squares and you roll an even number (2, 4, 6, 8, 10, or 12), count off your move as usual. If you roll an odd number (3, 5, 7, 9, or 11), you must go back to the police garage (square 2) and subtract 75.

Square 11: Don't count the off-on switch.

Square 12: Everyone else adds 50 to their score. You subtract 50 from your score for each of the other players in the game.

Square 17: Up to half past the hour, count the last hour. Half past or later, count the coming hour.

Square 20: If your display reads 1025, add 25. If your display reads 1025.3672, add 72.

Square 21: Your full given name with middle name but not nicknames.

Square 28: You select the player, who then adds your last two digits to his score as you subtract them from your own. (See note on square 20.)

Square 31: Let the others know of this instruction so there will be no confusion later.

Square 32: Windows, not window panes.

Square 35: All players (except you) subtract 10 from their scores. You add 10 to your score for each of the other players in the game.

Squares 39, 40, 41, and 42: You are insured only if you subtract 100. Place an elastic band around your marker if you do. The insurance refers to squares 62, 63, and 64.

Square 44: You must choose when you arrive. If you choose to subtract 200, place your marker in the left half of the square; if not, the right half. If you are in the left half you can go directly from square 44 to 59 as you count off your next roll of the dice. The use of the shortcut is possible only for players who land on this square.

Square 47: You pick the player you want to exchange with. He must exchange with you.

Square 48: The money must be in your pockets or with you now. Remember the decimal point: If you have $1.25, press 1.25, not 125. If 35¢, press .35, not 35.

Square 55: Let the others know of this instruction so there will be no confusion later. You may only recover your deposit if you pass **START** in the current round (see Reaching Start, below).

Squares 62, 63, and 64: Only players who have paid for insurance and placed an elastic band on their markers, while at squares 3, 39, 40, 41, or 42 in the current round may ignore the instructions.

Reaching START: Each round of the game ends as soon as one player reaches or passes **START**. Then all players must return to **START** and remove elastic bands if any. Remember your deposit if any. It is refunded only to the winner.

Disagreements: If a disagreement arises over how to interpret any of the instructions, the player whose turn it is shall decide in the fairest way he can. Usually, differences of opinion involve 1 or 2 points and are not worth worrying about.

1	**2**	**3**	**4**
START: First one to reach or pass here adds 500.*	**Police garage:** Subtract 75.	**Physical exam for insurance:** Subtract your age.*	**Household repairs** Subtract 50.
64 **Lawsuit:** See your lawyer (square 16), except if you are insured.*	**15** **See the vet:** Subtract 10 for each dog or cat you have.	**14** **Income tax:** Roll dice and subtract 10 times your throw.	**13** **Go on welfare:** Add each member of your family.
63 **Ulcer:** See your doctor (square 29), except if you are insured.*	**16** **Lawyer's office:** Subtract 100.	**17** **Time is money:** Add the time of day (nearest hour only).*	**18** **Education:** Subtract grade you are in.
62 **Heartburn:** See your doctor (square 29), except if you are insured.*	**29** **Doctor's office:** Subtract 100.	**28** **Pickpockets:** Give your last two digits to any player (as two-digit number).*	**27** **Sneakers wore out:** Subtract your shoe s
61 **Garbage strike:** Hold your nose and subtract 2.	**30** **Your birthday:** Add the date of month you were born.	**31** **Fed up:** Ignore instructions on next red square you reach.*	**32** **Fuel bill:** Subtract nu of windows and doors room.*
60 **Christmas bonus:** Add your age.	**43** **Broker's fee:** Divide by 1.03.	**42** If you want insurance, subtract 100. If not, do nothing.*	**41** If you want insuranc subtract 100. If not, nothing.*
59 **Phone bill:** Subtract last 2 digits in your phone number (as 2-digit number).	**44** **Political contribution:** Subtract 200 and take shortcut—or don't subtract and take long way.*	**45** **Inflation:** Multiply by .99.	**46** **Credit card interest** Subtract today's dat the month).
58 **Beauty parlor:** Subtract number of teeth on nearest comb.	**57** **Tax refund:** Roll dice and add 10 times your throw.	**56** **Interruptions:** Subtract the time of day (nearest hour only).	**55** **Security deposit:** Su tract 100. (You get it b you reach **START** firs

5 Stock dividend:* Multiply by 1.1.	**6** Keep up with the Joneses: Subtract from your total the last digit on everyone else's display.	**7** Rent due: Subtract 200.	**8** Big business deal: Add 100.*
12 Christmas: Give 50 to each player.*	**11** Car repairs: Subtract number of keys on your calculator.*	**10** Unemployment benefits: Flip coin. If heads, add 50. If tails, do nothing.	**9** Big business deal: Add 100.*
19 Bank interest: Multiply by 1.07.	**20** Harvest vegetable patch: Add last two digits on display (as two-digit number).*	**21** Business cards: Subtract number of letters in your full name.*	**22** Big business deal: Add 150.*
26 Win lottery: Add 10 times today's date (of the month).	**25** Social security: Add 100.	**24** Operating expenses: Subtract number on dice that got you here.	**23** Big business deal: Add 150.*
33 Monte Carlo vacation: Flip coin. If heads, multiply by .9. If tails, divide by .9.	**34** Electric bill: Subtract number of light bulbs in room.	**35** Win football pool: Take 10 from each player.*	**36** Big business deal: Add 200.*
40 If you want insurance, subtract 100. If not, do nothing.*	**39** If you want insurance, subtract 100. If not, do nothing.*	**38** Moonlighting: Add 100.	**37** Big business deal: Add 200.*
47 Trade in car: Change places with any player and add 70.*	**48** Allowance: Add money you have with you.*	**49** Royalty check: Add your height in inches.	**50** Big business deal: Add 250.*
54 Quiz show: Add number of letters in your mailing address.	**53** Charity: Subtract last digit on your display.	**52** Find money in street: Add number on dice that got you here.	**51** Big business deal: Add 250.*

TOW-AWAY ZONE

Tow-away zone: Go to police garage if you roll an odd number from any of the squares next to this zone.

TORMENT

Warning! Take a hint from the name of this puzzle. If you don't enjoy brainteasers, you had better pass on to the next page. But if you do like to test your wits, you may find this a fascinating challenge.

The puzzle is based on the letter-number code in the box below.

A = 1	G = 7	L = 12	Q = 17	V = 22
B = 2	H = 8	M = 13	R = 18	W = 23
C = 3	I = 9	N = 14	S = 19	X = 24
D = 4	J = 10	O = 15	T = 20	Y = 25
E = 5	K = 11	P = 16	U = 21	Z = 26
F = 6				

Using this code, you can take any word and write it in numbers rather than letters. For example, DOG would be written: 4 15 7, because D=4, O=15, and G=7. If you stop at this point, you can use the code to send secret messages. But to do the puzzle, take the code numbers, and use your calculator to **multiply** all the numbers out. For DOG, you would enter: **4 × 15 × 7 =**. The answer, 420, is the total value of the word DOG.

Now, the object of this puzzle is to find the word that gives you the highest possible total (99,999,999) **without overloading the calculator**. So DOG, with a value of 420, is a pretty poor word. Just as bad are very big words like

MULTIPLICATION, because they will overload the calculator.

The truth is, no one knows what word gives the best possible score. That's what makes this puzzle so interesting. A friend of ours thought he became the all-time winner with the word LIZZARDS (12 × 9 × 26 × 26 × 1 × 18 × 4 × 19) for an incredible score of 99,874,944. There was just one problem: He had spelled the word wrong, so it didn't count. A few of the words that give good totals are: pyramids, crocodile, octopus, drudgery.

Try to find some for yourself. You've done well if you can find a word, other than these, that totals over 60,000,000. You're quite good if you can pass 70,000,000, and it is outstanding if you find a word worth more than 80,000,000. Leave it at that if you wish. But the real challenge is to find a word that beats DRUDGERY (95,256,000). Sounds easy? Try it!

TIP: It helps to use a dictionary. Look for words of seven, eight, or nine letters. Be prepared to spend a while, because once you start, it's hard to quit. An answer is given on page 48, but it is not the only possible answer. At least one winning word is used in this book before the answer page.

MERRY-GO-ROUND

Though we use numbers in dozens of ways every day, we hardly ever stop to think about what they are in themselves. As you may have felt in playing many of the tricks and games in this book, numbers are sometimes very mysterious creatures. In fact, people have been fascinated by numbers for thousands of years, and electronic calculators have only added to the wonderment.

An especially tantalizing number is 7. It seems to be the key to many doors. There are seven colors in the rainbow, seven notes in the musical scale, seven days in the week, even seven dwarfs. But perhaps the most astonishing thing about the number 7 is what happens when you divide it into other numbers. Try these problems on your calculator and write the answers down:

$1 \div 7 = ?$ $2 \div 7 = ?$ $3 \div 7 = ?$ $4 \div 7 = ?$
$5 \div 7 = ?$ $6 \div 7 = ?$

Compare the sequence of the numbers in the answers. Amazing! Though each of the answers starts with a different number to the right of the decimal point, all contain the same numbers, and the numbers always follow each other in the same order. Eight always follows 2, 5 always follows 8, and on and on.

No number but 7 produces anything like this result. If you had a calculator with more than eight digits on the display, or if you were to solve the problem with pencil and paper, you would find another surprising thing: The sequence **142857** repeats itself endlessly in all the answers:

142857142857142857142857142857714

Here's a merry-go-round that never stops, though you can get on or off anywhere you want. The numbers even go up and down in a beautifully smooth rhythm, just like the horses on a real carousel: first up 3, down 2, up 6, then down 3, up 2, down 6. Hop on, and catch the golden ring if you can.

ANSWERS

Smarter Than You Think, page 14

In case you weren't sure, the words were:
heLLO, LESLIE, IGLOO, GOOSE EGG, GIGGLE, SIGh, GOSh, BILL, SLEIGh, BELLS, hOhOhO, ShOES, and hOLES.

Facts and Calculations Challenge, page 15.

a. $366 \times 13 = 4758$
b. $- 1666 = 3092$
c. $+ 5280 = 8372$
d. $\div 52 = 161$
e. $\times 1492 = 240,212$
f. $- 16 = 240,196$
g. $\div 212 = 1133$
h. $+ 7 = 1140$
i. $\times 26 \times 26 = 770.640$
j. $\div 12 = 64,220$
k. $- 1969 = 62.251$
l. $+ 2000 = 64,251$
m. $- 28 = 64,223$
n. $+ 1 = 64,224$
o. $\div 144 = 446$
p. $- 360 = 86$
q. $+ 14 = 100$
r. $\div 100 = 1$
The answer is 1.

Quiz For Nimble Fingers, page 18.

(Note: Some calculators are more accurate than others. In answers that contain decimal points, your last digit or two on the right may be different from the answer given. But if the rest of your answer is the same, consider it correct.)

1. 12369874 (Surprise!)
2. 593.5607 −
3. 0.8888888 −
4. 4.15625
5. 12
6. 17
7. 787.5
8. 423.21427
9. 3.96
10. 155.3125
11. 51.476188
12. 375
13. 40.8
14. 14.914285
15. 25.666666
16. 4.2777778 −
17. 2.111112 −
18. 0.52
19. 20
20. 42.5
21. 100
22. 123.09375
23. 4.2361111
24. 18.618181
25. 17.466667
26. 774501.47
27. 21.963917
28. 14142
29. 1001

Calculator Maze, page 16

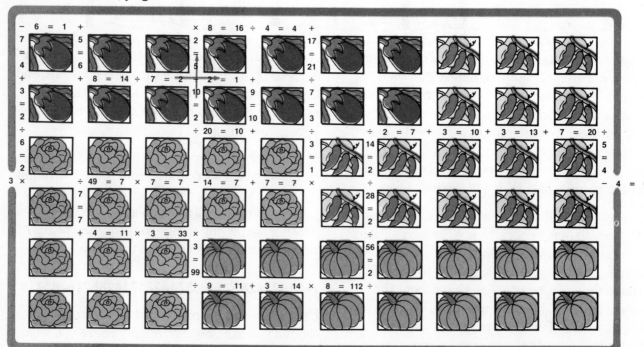

Torment, page 46

One possible answer is: TORMENT ($20 \times 15 \times 18 \times 13 \times 5 \times 14 \times 20 = 98,280,000$).